PIANO SOLO

OLA GJEILO
DAWN

Dawn is available from Decca Classics (4852954).
shop.decca.com

Edited by Dan Rollison and James Welland
Music by Ola Gjeilo

ISBN 978-1-70518-331-1

CHESTER MUSIC
part of **WiseMusic**Group

EXCLUSIVELY DISTRIBUTED BY

HAL•LEONARD®

Visit Hal Leonard Online at
www.halleonard.com

Contact us:
Hal Leonard
7777 West Bluemound Road
Milwaukee, WI 53213
Email: info@halleonard.com

In Europe, contact:
Hal Leonard Europe Limited
1 Red Place
London, W1K 6PL
Email: info@halleonardeurope.com

In Australia, contact:
Hal Leonard Australia Pty. Ltd.
4 Lentara Court
Cheltenham, Victoria, 3192 Australia
Email: info@halleonard.com.au

CONTENTS

DAYBREAK

Ola Gjeilo

NEW MOON

Ola Gjeilo

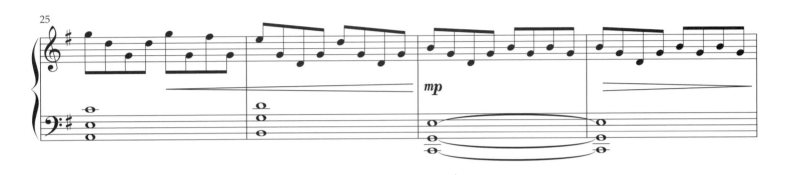

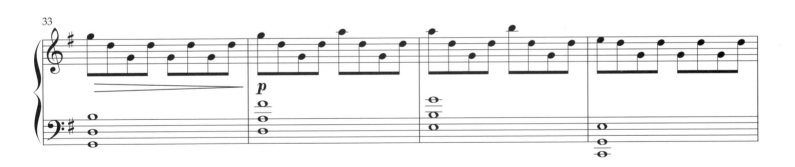

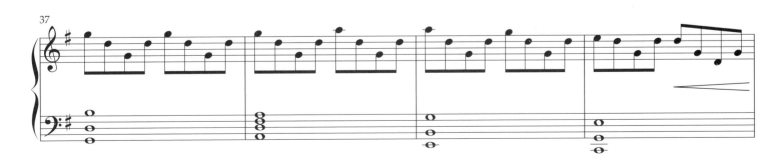

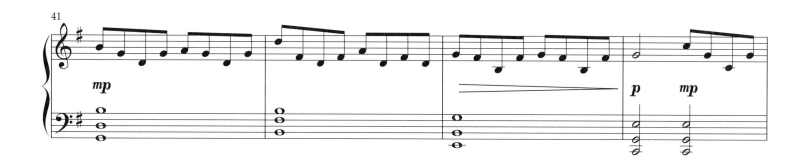

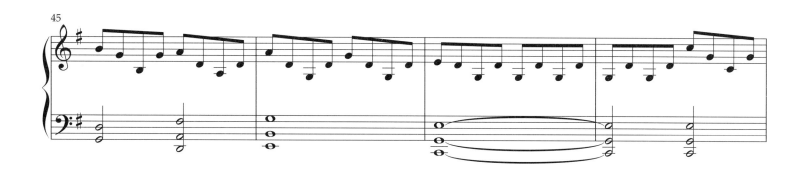

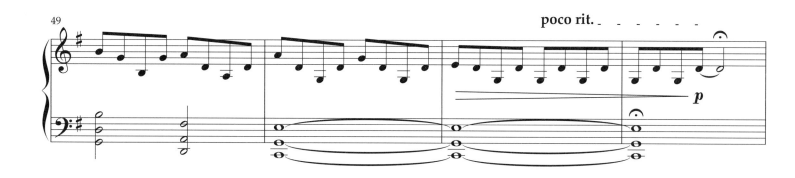

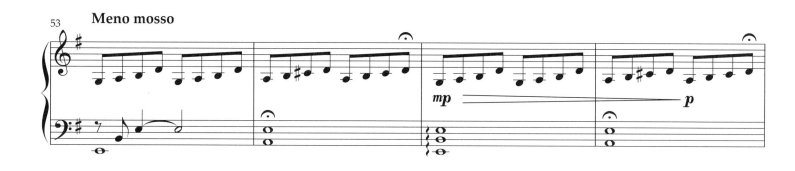

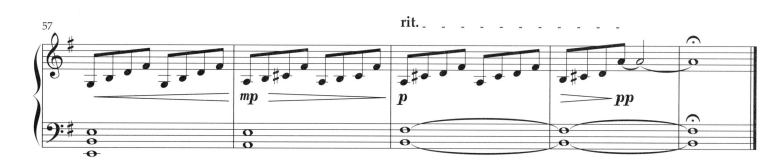

ETERNITY

Ola Gjeilo

SUN PRELUDE

Ola Gjeilo

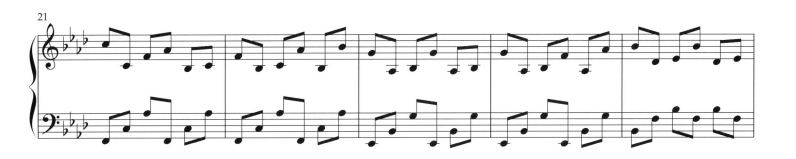

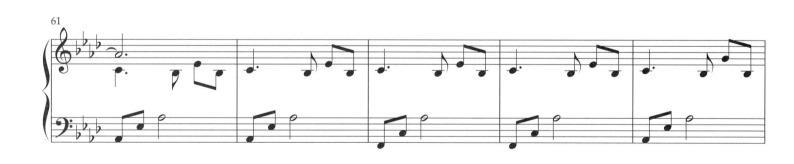

rit. _ _ _ _ _ _ _ _ _ _ _ _

BLUE

Ola Gjeilo

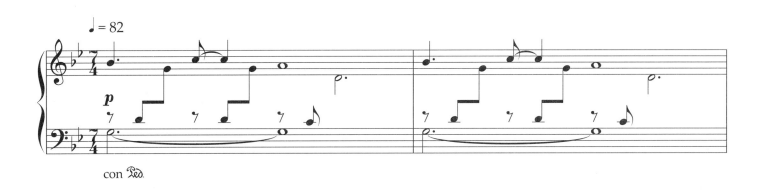

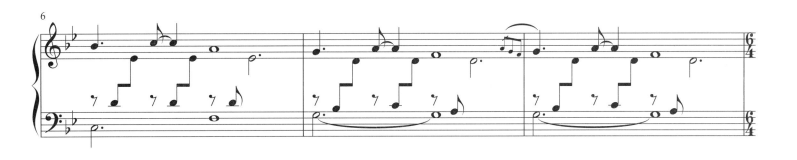

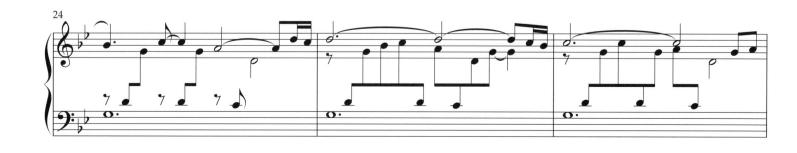

MANHATTAN SUNRISE

Ola Gjeilo

HOMEBOUND

Ola Gjeilo

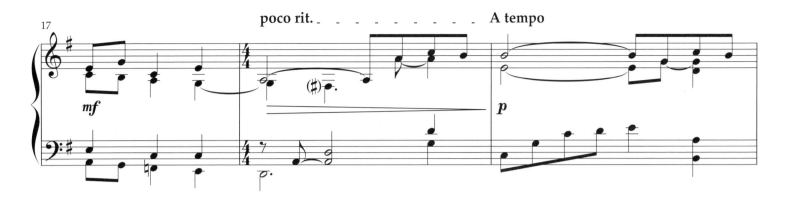

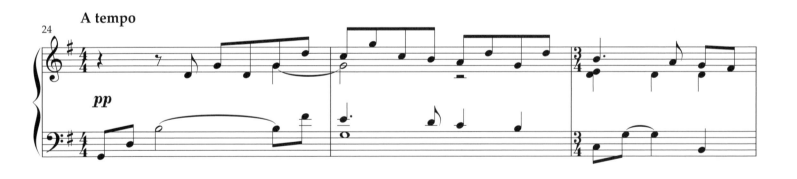

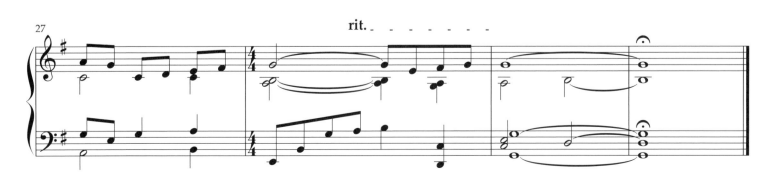

CLARITY

Ola Gjeilo

MONTANA

Ola Gjeilo

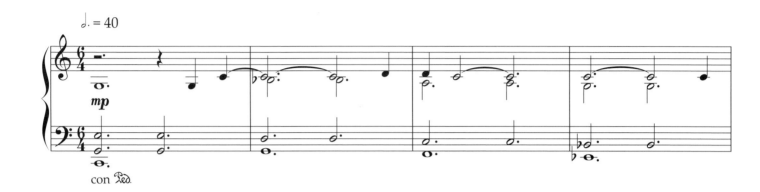

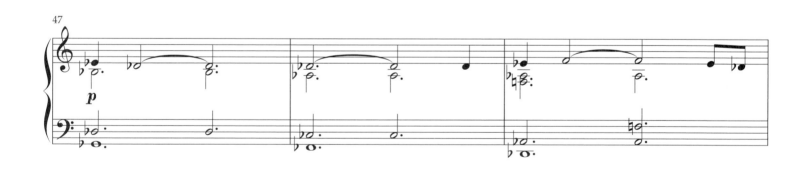

This page has intentionally been left blank to facilitate page turns.

ORANGE SOUND

Ola Gjeilo

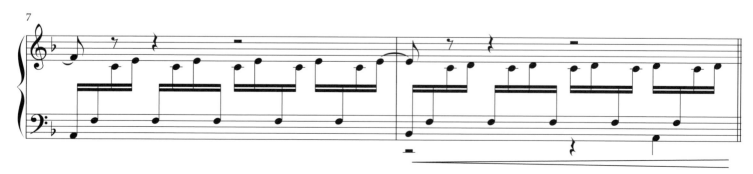

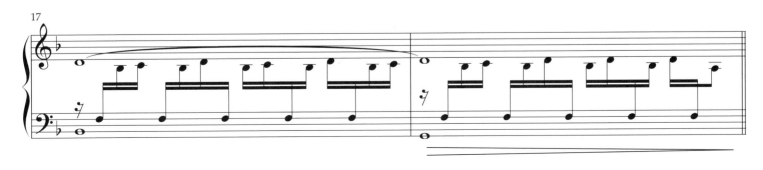

poco rit. _ _ _ _

STASIS

Ola Gjeilo

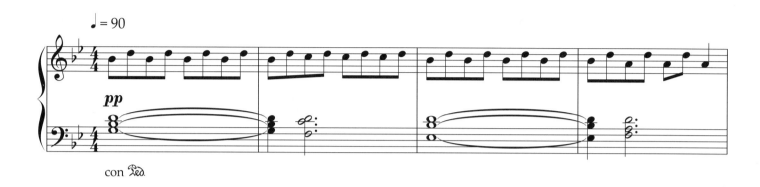

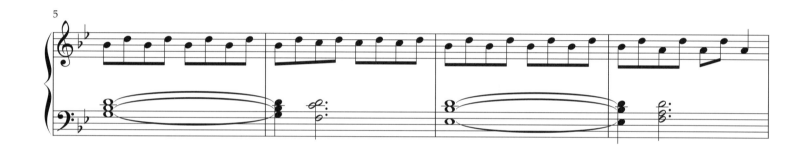

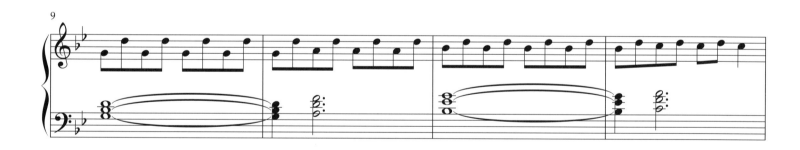

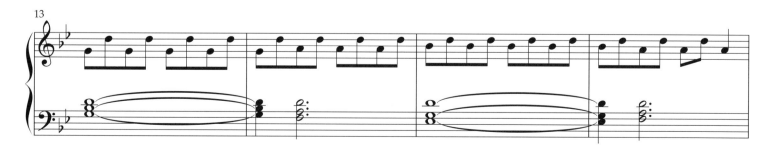

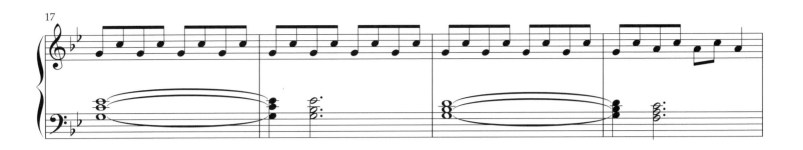

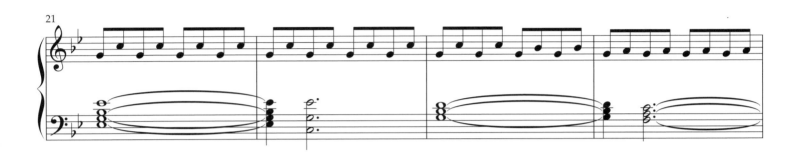

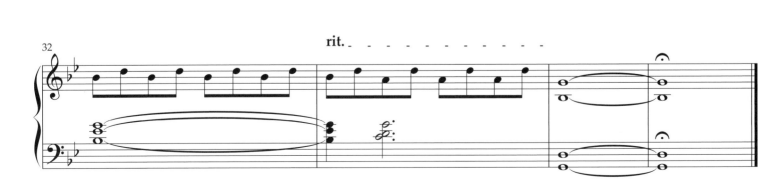

CHRONICLES

Ola Gjeilo

ORIGIN

Ola Gjeilo

SILVER LINING

Ola Gjeilo

DAWN SKY

Ola Gjeilo

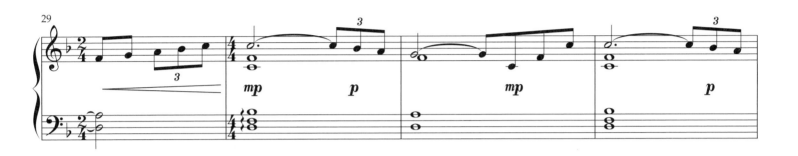

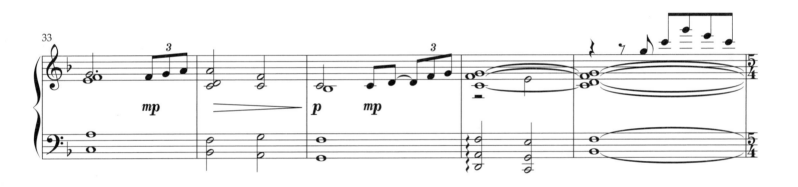

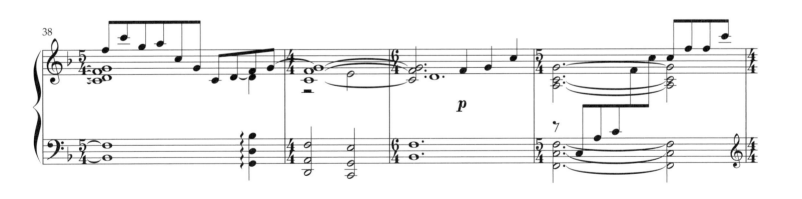

FIRST LIGHT

Ola Gjeilo

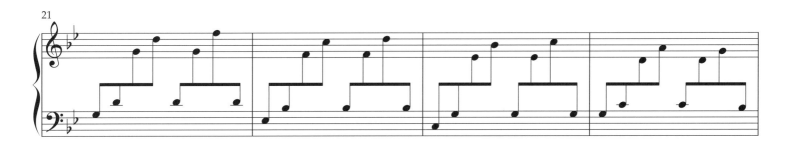

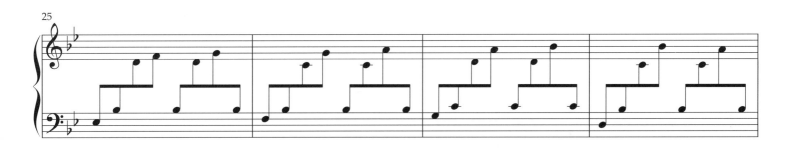

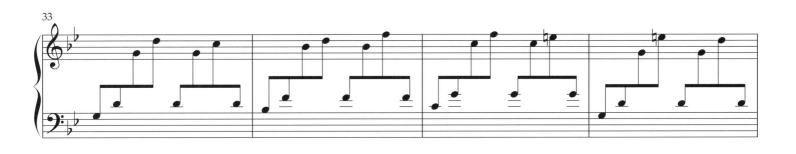

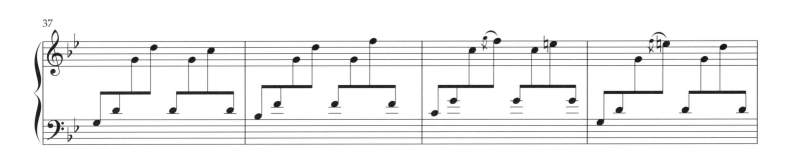

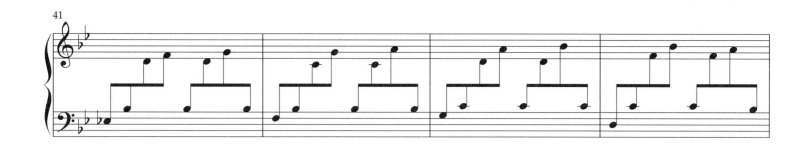

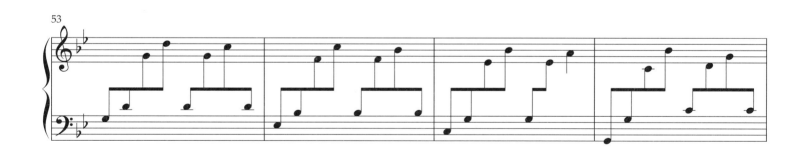

SHINE

Ola Gjeilo

rit. _ _ _ _ _ _ _ _ _